Books by Kids!

Helping Young Children Create Their Own Books

by Karen Nelsen

Fearon Teacher Aids
A Paramount Communications Company

Editorial Director: Virginia L. Murphy
Editor: Lisa Schwimmer
Copyeditor: Kristin Eclov
Cover Design and Illustration: Teena Remer
Inside Design and Illustration: Teena Remer

ISBN 0-86653-930-1

Printed in the United States of America

1.9 8 7 6 5 4 3 2

Contents

• • • • • • • • • • • • • • • • •

• • • • • • • • • • • • • • • • •

Introduction

● ● ● ● ● ● ● ● ● ● ● ● ● ● ● ● ● ● ● ●

Primary-grade children have an innate curiosity and a strong desire to learn. *Books by Kids!*, a program to help children write their own books, provides a strong literature-based environment and an incentive for young children to not only succeed, but thrive intellectually and academically. Creating a classroom of authors and illustrators helps build self-esteem in children, fosters good work habits, and helps children develop strong academic skills.

It is a misconception that nonwriters cannot "write" books. Classroom books can be started on the first day of school, or at any time during the year, and completed in a relatively short period of time. For example, comparison books, the first writing unit in this resource guide, provide a logical way to begin the writing process in the classroom. These books are easy to write, very versatile, and easily integrated into any curriculum. Completion of a comparison book during the first few weeks of school will give children a positive sense of accomplishment. This early success will also set the stage for developing more in-depth writing as the year progresses.

The Format

Books by Kids! provides writing units for five different types of books that can be written by young children—comparison books, alphabet books, books based on reading skills, fiction books, and nonfiction books—as well as illustration ideas and topic suggestions appropriate for your classroom. The books presented in this guide are intended to be written as a class, with each child contributing his or her own unique ideas or pages. You may decide, however, to have children make individual books or small-group books instead. Each choice is possible with the resources provided. Within each writing unit are four steps that will help guide you and the children through the entire writing process.

The first section of each unit introduces you to the concept of the particular unit and how each unit will benefit your students. The four steps are as follows:

✎ *Getting Started* begins the writing process—selecting topics, setting up the work environment, and so on.

✎ *Suggested Topics* provides writing ideas for each unit. You may use the topics listed or challenge children to think of ideas of their own.

✎ The *Brainstorming/Prewriting Activities* section includes suggestions and ideas that help children think about the topics before they start to actually write their books. These activities are probably the most critical component of the writing process. Brainstorming and the charting of these ideas helps children prepare for the task of writing by providing the ideas and concepts required to actually write the classroom books. Brainstorming during the prewriting process encourages group interaction and cooperative idea-sharing in a non-competitive environment. Children who learn to brainstorm ideas at an early stage in their writing development usually become more creative writers. Plus, those students with weaker skills and limited expressive language ability will benefit from the shared ideas of their classmates.

Bringing It All Together gets down to the actual bookmaking. Children copy their ideas generated during the brainstorming and charting sessions onto their papers and then illustrate their pages. Expansion ideas and challenges for more advanced children are provided as well. Keep in mind that this last section does not stand on its own. The four steps within each of the writing units fit together and are actually all a part of the entire writing process.

Illustrations are an integral part in the development of a class book. Illustrating ideas can be discussed in conjunction with the brainstorming and prewriting process, but completed during the assembling of the book itself. For young children, especially, a book is not complete without colorful, eye-catching pictures. Illustrations help keep a child's interest, as well as offer clues about the story text. The ideas on pages 61-68 present several different illustrating methods. Information is also provided to help determine which techniques are best to use for the children's different capabilities.

Initiating a book-writing program in your primary classroom ties together all the important elements of literature-based instruction, curriculum integration, cooperative learning, and active student participation. Children who are exposed to good literature and poetry enjoy using their favorite books and authors as catalysts for writing on their own. In addition, participation in a book-writing program helps children gain confidence and expand their writing capabilities

Using Books by Kids in the Classroom

Make your classroom an easy place to think and write. Set up a resource center in the room with picture dictionaries and reference materials related to the chosen topics. Give the children time to look through the reference materials. Encourage children to bring their favorite books from home as well.

Books children write and illustrate themselves often become classroom favorites. They are read and reread until the children know them by heart. Even nonreaders will be able to take these books from the classroom library and "read" their own pages of text. Young children can also use the illustrations to help identify the words.

As children in the classroom develop their own libraries, their enthusiasm for writing will grow. The progression from writing comparison books to independent writing is gradual, but the children's involvement and eagerness to write will be greatly increased. Their constant success and your positive feedback will show the children that there is no limit to what they can create.

Unit 1: Comparison Books

About Comparison Books

Comparison books require children to draw from their own knowledge and prior experience in comparing objects— for example, an apple is as red as a rose, a ball is as round as the moon, and so on. Teaching comparison skills to young children involves helping children discover what certain objects have in common.

The simplest comparison book to make with children is one where you provide an object for the children to compare things to. For example, if the topic is "An Apple Is As Red As…," each child may make his or her own comparison—An Apple Is As Red As a Rose, An Apple Is As Red As a Tomato, An Apple Is As Red As a Fire Truck, and so on. Topics can be preselected by you or by the children themselves.

Comparison books provide a simple method of getting primary children involved in creative activities from the first day they arrive at school. Children can be encouraged to identify everything they can think of that has a certain characteristic—a red color, for example—an apple, a fire truck, or a stop sign. Explain to the children that each of the objects has something in common with the others—in this case, the color red.

Comparison books can be used to help teach young children the concepts of size, shape, color, texture, and so on. They can also be used to teach same and different, as well as help children learn to categorize. For example, the class can create a series of books based on sizes of objects—small objects, medium objects, and large. Comparison books can be written about any topic the children are familiar with.

Getting Started

Select a topic that can be integrated into the curriculum, such as sizes, shapes, buildings in the neighborhood, foods, pets, and so on. Refer to the suggested topics on page 11 for ideas. With nonwriters, start by brainstorming ideas for color and shape comparison books. Examples of book titles might include:

> An Apple Is As Red As...
> The School Bus Is As Yellow As...
> A Ball Is As Round As...
> An Elephant Is As Big As...

Upper primary children who are capable of writing independently may want to choose topics of their own. They can work individually or in small groups. For example, if a class is studying measurement, each child can select a nonstandard unit of measurement and find other objects of approximate size. Give children several objects to use as measuring units, such as crayons, chalkboard erasers, or notebooks. Ask the children to walk around the classroom and find other objects that are about the same size. Titles might include:

> A Straw Is As Big As...
> A Paper Clip Is As Big As ...
> My Math Book Is As Big As...

Groups of older children can also work cooperatively to write a book composed of different chapters. For example, a book about seasons could be written comparing each season with something different—Spring Is As Pretty As..., Summer Is As Hot As..., Fall Is As Colorful As..., Winter Is As Cold As..., and so on. Each group can be responsible for a different chapter.

Suggested Topics

Comparison books are easily integrated into any curriculum or content area. The list of topics can include colors, shapes, sizes, holidays, seasons, feelings, and so on. Older children can use comparison books to study specific content areas, such as science, social studies, or health. The following list of topics can be used as titles for comparison books.

An Apple Is As Red As...
I Am As Big As...
Johnny Appleseed Walked As Far As...

A Pumpkin Is As Heavy As...
The Fall Moon Is As Orange As...
I Can Throw a Football As Far As...

A Turkey Is As Brown As...
Fall Leaves Are As Colorful As...
The Mayflower Voyage Was As Difficult As ...

Snow Is As Soft As...
A Christmas Tree Is As Green As...
Santa Is As Chubby As...
Hibernating Animals Are As Quiet As...
A Menorah Is As Bright As...

The Winter Sky Is As Blue As...
A Snowman Is As Cold As...
A Polar Bear Is As Fuzzy As...

A Valentine Is As Pink As...
Candy Is As Sweet As...
The Presidents Are As Wise As...

The Weather Is As Stormy As...
A Leprechaun Is As Tricky As...
A Pot of Gold Is As Shiny As...
A Kite Can Fly As High As...

Spring Flowers Are As Pretty As...
A Baseball Is As Round As...
A Mouse Is As Quiet As...
A Tree Is As Green As...

Insects Are As Numerous As...
The Sun Is As Hot As...
A School Bus Is As Yellow As...

A Bee Is As Busy As...
A Feather Is As Light As...
The Night Is As Dark As...

Brainstorming/Prewriting Activities

The brainstorming/prewriting activities are probably the most critical component of the writing process. These activities help children prepare for the task of writing by providing the ideas and concepts required to actually write the classroom books. Charting children's ideas (on chart paper, butcher paper, or the bulletin board) provides the source from which the children choose ideas as they actually sit down and write their books or book pages. Use the following activities, as well as other activities that may appeal to you, to help children brainstorm and expand their ideas. Many options are provided here so that you may choose those that will be most appropriate for your class. Each activity can be used independently or combined with other activities to help children brainstorm text for their comparison books.

Starting Point

Encourage the children to think of as many items as they can that are comparable to the comparison book topic the children have selected. For example, if the topic is objects that are big, have the children name all the items they can think of that are as big as the preselected topic. For example:

> A Car Is As Big As an Elephant
> A Car Is As Big As a Hippopotamus

Write the children's ideas on a large sheet of chart paper. Have each child sign his or her name next to his or her idea. If someone has difficulty thinking of an object, encourage the rest of the class to give suggestions and encourage the child to choose his or her favorite. Each child should have his or her own line of text written on the chart.

A Car Is As Big As...	Name
an Elephant	Jerome
a House	Willie
a Giraffe	Jessica
An Apple Is As Red As...	Name
a Barn	Roger
a Tomato	Lewis
a Rose	Sally

Once the list is finished, post it in a prominent location in the classroom. Encourage the children to become familiar with the text by reading the chart periodically throughout the day. Invite each child to read his or her own line of text independently. This charted list will later become the text for the children's book pages.

A Class Walk

Take a walk around the neighborhood, school, or playground. Help the children identify objects that can be compared to their chosen topic, such as an apple is as red as a fire engine. Keep track of all the objects the class sees that are red. Point out that some objects are all red, such as a tomato, while other objects are partially red, such as the lettering on a mailbox. Help the children become critical observers of detail by pointing out the various shades of red. For example, the bricks on a chimney are not the same color red as is a geranium.

Bring an example of the red object you are comparing along on the walk. To better illustrate the differences in colors, hold up the red apple next to as many red objects as possible, such as stop signs, bricks, fire hydrants, and so on. Point out the differences in the shades of red. Be sensitive to the fact that some children may not be able to see the color differences. The more detail the children observe, the easier it will be for the children to brainstorm about the topic and illustrate their books creatively. Record the children's responses during the walk. Upon returning to the classroom, discuss what the children observed on their outing and write their responses on chart paper (see "Starting Point" on page 12).

Box Drawings

Making box drawings can help children come up with creative ideas for their comparison books. Fold large pieces of drawing paper into eight boxes for each child. Older children may want to fold their own papers. Invite the children to choose eight items that can be compared to a selected topic to include in their set of boxes. Have the children draw one item in each box. Encourage the children to be observant and include details in their drawings. Help children make their drawings as identifiable as possible. Ask the children to label their pictures. Don't worry about correct spelling at this point. Chart the children's responses.

Create a Collage

Help children make collages from magazine pictures of comparable items. Collect old magazines and catalogs and keep them in a central location for the children to use. Discuss with the children whether they would like to work on collages individually, in small groups, or as a class. Encourage the children working individually or in small groups to create small collages on construction paper. If the collage is a class project, cover a bulletin board with butcher paper. Have the children cut out all the magazine pictures of the items. Glue or staple the pictures to the collage. Creating visual images of how items can be compared will help the children as they brainstorm ideas for their comparison book pages. Write children's ideas on chart paper (see "Starting Point" on page 12).

Comparable Lists

Encourage the children to work with their parents or guardians to make lists of comparable items at home. Younger children can use either pictures or words. It would also be helpful if parents or guardians labeled their children's pictures for them. Have the children bring their lists to school and share them with the class. On a large sheet of lined chart paper, record the children's responses and display them in the classroom. Encourage children to bring in an item from home on their lists to show the class. For example, if children are comparing red items, they could bring in a red mitten, red raisin box, red flower, and so on. Display the objects in the classroom.

Read to the Class

Select books from the school or public library that can be integrated into the topic chosen for a class comparison book. Discuss the books and how they relate to the topic. If the comparison book being written is about objects that are red, for example, you could read *Red* by Gabrielle Woolfitt or Kathy Stinson's *Red Is Best* (see the bibliography on page 70). Children may get ideas for their book pages from the selected books read in class.

Children's Notebooks

Children who are writers, even at the early stages of writing, can use a paper and pencil to write down their own ideas during brainstorming sessions. Encourage the children to keep track of their ideas in notebooks. This will help prevent duplicating ideas and also provide a record for any child who is having difficulty writing. It is also helpful to keep a written record of each child's ideas as he or she offers them aloud. Keep a notebook handy during class brainstorming sessions. Copy the list on a large sheet of chart paper and display it in the classroom. Help the children edit their work by comparing what they have written to the text written on the chart.

Bringing It All Together

The following steps help children incorporate all of the preceding activities as they write and illustrate their comparison book or books.

1. Help children make a title page that includes the book title, class name, and date.

2. Give each child a clean sheet of writing or drawing paper for his or her comparison book pages.

3. Help each child copy his or her comparison words or sentence from the brainstorming and charting sessions on the bottom of his or her sheet of paper. At the very earliest stages of writing, it may be necessary for you to print each child's text. Ask each child to read his or her text with you as it is written.

4. Encourage each child to illustrate his or her ideas (see pages 61-68 for illustrating ideas). Help children make the drawings as easy to identify as possible. Help young children "read" the text written on their pages once again after the pages are illustrated.

5. Have the children sign their names on their pages.

6. Staple the pages of the book together with the title page on top. Or you may want to punch holes in the pages along the side or the top and tie the book together with string or yarn.

7. If you wish, help the children make a cover for the class book. You can use a variety of materials, such as cardboard, tagboard, fabric, and so on.

Expanding

- For children who are able to go a step further, encourage the use of adjectives and descriptive phrases in their comparison words or sentences. Ask simple questions about each child's item to find out more information.

     An Apple Is As Red As a Big Cow Barn
     A Car Is As Big As a Gray Circus Elephant

- Encourage children at the upper primary levels to copy their text independently. Give each child a sheet of paper with a line drawn across the bottom. The line will provide a guide on which to write their text. After the text is written in, invite the children to illustrate their pages and sign their names.

Challenge

Older children may wish to work on comparison books independently or in small groups. They can work on assigned topics or be encouraged to develop topics of their own. At this level of writing, you can act as advisor and editor. Meet with the children and ask questions that will expand their ideas and add description to their narratives. For example, if a child is working on a book entitled "Winter Is As Cold As…," he or she might use "ice" as one of his or her comparisons. Ask questions similar to the following:

     Where is the ice (at the North Pole, on the window, in the refrigerator)?
     What form is the ice in (iceberg, ice cube, icicle)?
     What does the ice look like (sparkling, glimmering, shiny)?

The child's resulting text might be:

     Winter Is As Cold As a Sparkling Icicle at the North Pole
     Winter Is As Cold As a Glimmering Ice Cube in the Refrigerator

Unit 2: Alphabet Books

About Alphabet Books

Alphabet books follow a simple format that most children are already familiar with. Even children who have not been exposed to alphabet books quickly understand the alphabetical sequence and feel comfortable in brainstorming and writing this type of book on their own.

Alphabet books can be written using a variety of techniques and subject matter. They can be as simple or complex as appropriate for the children. The simplest alphabet books are created from alphabetical lists of non-related words. The more complex books are written using a sentence format.

Invite children to use primary reference materials, if appropriate, as resources as they write their alphabet books. Show the children how a picture or elementary dictionary is arranged in alphabetical order, then invite children to practice using the dictionary to find words that begin with a certain letter. For example:

F—flower, flute, fly
G—galaxy, garden, garter snake

Simple alphabet books can be started at an early stage in a young child's development. They can be written with increasing complexity as the children build and strengthen their reading and writing skills. Upper primary children with stronger writing skills can be given the guidance necessary to work on their pages independently or in small groups.

Getting Started

Determine which type of alphabet book will best meet the needs and level of the children in your classroom—non-related words, adjectives before nouns, or sentence formats (see the suggested topics on pages 20-21 for ideas). When writing an alphabet book with nonwriters, or early in the year with upper primary children, it is best to start with a simple format. Basic alphabet books can be written from a list of non-related words. As a class activity, encourage the children to name as many objects as they can think of for each letter of the alphabet. Record the children's responses on the chalkboard. Encourage the children to skip letters if they can't think of an example.

> apple
> ball
> cat

Slightly more complicated books can include an adjective before each noun. As a class, make a list of several adjectives for each letter of the alphabet. Encourage the children to choose an adjective to use for each letter.

> awesome apple
> bouncing ball
> cute cat

Upper primary children or those children with experience writing may want to brainstorm alphabet books using a sentence format. The simplest of these formats requires only the first word in the sentence to be in alphabetical order.

> Alligators are reptiles.
> Birds can fly.
> Cats have whiskers.

As alphabet books become more complex, the children can be challenged to brainstorm three-word sentences in which the first and last words begin with the same letter.

> Alligators eat apples.
> Birds eat berries.
> Cats like catnip.

When working with experienced writers, alphabet books can become even more detailed and complex. Books written at more advanced levels can be integrated with different curriculum areas and will require some content knowledge, as well as group research and brainstorming. Each child can be assigned an individual letter of the alphabet. Have the class choose whether to work independently or in small groups. The children in small groups can work on several different letters of the alphabet.

The Universe
Asteroids are rock fragments.
Big Dipper is a constellation.
Constellations are star pictures.
Daring astronauts explore space.

Alphabet books based on specific content areas will require a little ingenuity and the use of adjectives or adverbs to complete the alphabetical requirements.

Suggested Topics

Alphabet books are easily integrated into any curriculum or content area. The list of topics can include animals, plants, social-studies subjects, maps, and so on. Older children can use alphabet books to study specific content areas, such as science, social studies, or health. The following are topic suggestions for a variety of alphabet books:

Lists of non-related words—apple, ball, cat

Adjectives before nouns—awesome apple, bouncing ball, cute cat

Three-word sentence format adding a color word after each noun—apples are red, balls are blue, cats are black

Alphabet books about a specific topic with one word or a simple phrase on each page:

Foods—apple, banana, carrot
People's names—Amy, Billy, Carl
Animals—alligator, bird, cat
Objects—airplane, boat, coffeepot
Nature's creations—acorn, beetle, cloud

Alphabet books using simple sentences:

Silly animals and foods—alligators eat apples, birds eat bananas, cats eat carrots
Funny animal homes—ants live in airplanes, bees live in baskets, caterpillars live in clocks
Silly people—Alan ate ants, Betty bounces bread, Carl cuts caps

Books using adjectives to describe any animal from A to Z—elephants are awesome, elephants are big, elephants are cantankerous

Alphabet tongue twisters—all alligators are angry at ants; big, brown bears bring blue balloons to the beach; cute, cuddly cats can color caterpillars with crayons

Asking silly "What If" questions—what if airplanes had antlers, what if balls had brains, what if cats had cameras

All about animals—alligators are reptiles,
birds can fly, cats are independent

All about plants—acorns are seeds of oak trees,
beautiful flowers grow on some plants, cactus
grows in the desert

Native Americans—America's first inhabitants were
Native Americans, buffalo were a source of food
for the Plains Indians, Cherokee Indians first lived
on the East Coast

Map skills—atlases help us learn about maps,
bays are bodies of water, continents are large
masses of land

The Universe—asteroids are rock fragments,
Big Dipper is a constellation, constellations are
star pictures

Brainstorming/Prewriting Activities

The brainstorming/prewriting activities are probably the most critical component of the writing process. These activities help children prepare for the task of writing by providing the ideas and concepts required to actually write the classroom books. Charting children's ideas (on chart paper, butcher paper, or the bulletin board) provides the source from which the children choose ideas as they actually sit down and write their books or book pages. Use the following activities, as well as other activities that may appeal to you, to help children brainstorm and expand their ideas. Many options are provided here so that you may choose those that will be most appropriate for your class. Each activity can be used independently or combined with other activities to help children brainstorm text for their alphabet books.

Starting Point

Choose a topic for an alphabet book—silly animals and foods, for example. Use large chart paper and write each letter of the alphabet from A to Z on separate lines of the chart. Have the children begin by brainstorming animals or foods that begin with the letter "A." One child may be able to think of the word "alligator," but unable to think of a food. Another child may think of the word "apple." The joint effort will result in the text "Alligators eat apples." Encourage the children to brainstorm more than one animal or food for each letter. Write the children's suggestions on the chalkboard. Have the children vote for their favorite choices before copying the text onto the chart.

A—alligator, ant, anteater, aardvark, apples, applesauce
B—badger, bunny, billy goat, bubblegum, bananas

The class may be unable to think of words for one or more of the letters. Skip those letters and return to them at another time. Post the incomplete chart in the classroom to allow the children to become familiar with the text. Encourage children to use resource guides, such as picture dictionaries or alphabet books, to look for words during their independent time. Encourage the children to look for alphabet words at home and talk to their parents or guardians about possible words for the text as well. The charted list will later become the text for the children's book pages.

Share several alphabet books with the class to help give the children ideas for finishing the chart (see the bibliography on pages 70-71). Provide picture dictionaries for the children to use as well. If necessary, introduce the use of adjectives or adverbs in order to complete the text.

unusual eggplants
x-rayed onions
zippy peppers

Letter Collages

Assign each child or small group of children a letter of the alphabet. As a class, discuss some possible picture ideas for each letter. Write the list on the chalkboard or on chart paper. Then ask the children to look for pictures of objects in magazines, newspapers, and catalogs that begin with each letter.

Invite children to cut out a variety of magazine pictures of objects for each letter, such as an apple, ball, cat, and dinosaur. As a class, invite the children to think of other examples for each letter, too. Encourage the children to create collages using magazine pictures or their own artwork. Each collage should only have pictures that begin with a certain letter. Encourage children to cut out different sizes of letters and include them in the collage as well. Once the collages are finished, display them around the classroom. Invite the children to use the collage to help them brainstorm words or sentences for their alphabet books (see "Starting Point" on page 21).

Alphabet Drawings

Give each child a piece of drawing paper with his or her letter of the alphabet printed on it. Make the letter at least six inches (15.2 cm) high. Ask each child to draw something that begins with his or her letter of the alphabet using the letter as part of the picture.

Or, give the children outlines of block letters and invite them to draw pictures of objects that begin with each letter, such as a Z full of zebras or an F full of fish.

Invite the children to trade letters or help each other brainstorm picture ideas. If a child has difficulty incorporating the letter into his or her drawing, invite that child to draw on the opposite side of the paper without using the preprinted letter in the picture. Ask the children to share their completed pictures with their classmates. Show the children the alphabet book *Anno's Alphabet* (see the bibliography on page 70) as a good example of incorporating letters into an illustration. Invite children to use their drawings as a basis for their written text. Write children's choices on chart paper.

Letter Sentences

Begin each day by brainstorming silly sentences or tongue twisters. These sentences may be simple and limited to as few as three words, or they may be more complex as the children grow more sophisticated at brainstorming and writing. Read excerpts from *Animalia* (see the bibliography on page 70) to show the children how really silly sentences sound. Challenge older children to create more complicated sentences as well. Simple silly sentences might include:

> Alan eats ants.
> Betty bounces bread.
> Carl cuts caps.

Complex silly sentences might include:

> All alligators are angry at ants.
> Big, brown bears bring blue balloons to the beach.
> Cute, cuddly cats can color caterpillars with crayons.

Using More Complex Alphabet Words

Invite children to choose a letter of the alphabet. Or, assign each child a specific letter. Give the children an appropriate amount of time to find as many words as possible for their letters. For example, a child who has been assigned the letter "C" may automatically think of the word "cat." Encourage the child to use primary reference books and look for other "C" words, too.

> caterpillar
> chameleon
> cougar
> canary
> cheetah
> centipede

Give the children several days to come up with words for their letters. Have each student read his or her alphabet words aloud for the class. Record the responses on a large sheet of chart paper. Write each child's name by his or her responses. For children who are having difficulty finding words to represent their letters, encourage the class to help by brainstorming word suggestions.

An Alphabet Game

Start at the beginning of the alphabet and ask the first child to name something that begins with the letter "A." The second child then names something that begins with "B," and so on. If a child is unable to think of a word for a letter, allow the child to skip the turn by saying "pass." Continue around the room as many times as necessary to complete the alphabet. As the children become more proficient at this activity, they may want to time themselves to see if they can complete the alphabet within a specific time frame. The children might say:

> alligator
> beach ball
> cat
> dog
> pass (go to the next person)
> egg

Invite children to use the words named during the alphabet game for the alphabet book text.

Reading Alphabet Books

Read several alphabet books to the class (see the bibliography on pages 70-71). Discuss the style each author used to write the book, such as using non-related words, adjectives before the nouns, or a sentence format. Children will soon be able to identify books that are alphabetized using pictures, animals, and people's names. Ask the children to decide whether each book is factual or fiction. Point out the type of text used by each author, whether it's single word, phrases, complete sentences, or rhymes. Children may get ideas for their book pages from the selected books read in class. If so, chart the children's responses. Examples of the different alphabet book styles include:

> non-related words—*Anno's Alphabet* and *Alphabatics*
>
> adjectives before nouns—*Chicka Chicka Boom Boom* and *Fun from A to Z*
>
> sentence format—*Animalia* and *Alaska ABC Book*

Bringing It All Together

The following steps help children incorporate all of the preceding activities as they write and illustrate their alphabet book or books.

1. Before beginning to write the text for an alphabet book, it is necessary to decide whether or not each child should have the responsibility for creating a specific line of text or if the children will work together. First attempts at alphabet books written with nonwriters are easier to "write" as a group where the children work together and combine their ideas. Collaborative work is very effective at the lower primary levels.

2. As a class, decide on a title for the alphabet book. Help children make a title page for the book that includes the book title, class name, and date.

3. Give each child a clean sheet of writing or drawing paper for his or her alphabet book pages.

4. Help each child copy his or her alphabet sentence or word from the brainstorming and charting sessions at the bottom of the sheet of paper. At the very earliest stages of writing, it may be necessary for you to print each child's line of text. Ask each child to read his or her line of text with you as it is written on the page.

5. Encourage each child to illustrate his or her ideas (see pages 61-68 for illustrating ideas). Help children make the drawings as easy to identify as possible. This will help young children "read" the text written on their pages once again after the pages are illustrated.

6. Have the children sign their names on their pages.

7. Staple the pages of the book together with the title page on top. Or you may want to punch holes in the pages along the side or the top and tie the book together with string or yarn.

8. If you wish, help the children make a cover for the class book. You can use a variety of materials, such as cardboard, tagboard, fabric, and so on.

Expanding

- Encourage children in the upper primary levels to copy their entire lines of text independently. Give each child a sheet of paper with a line drawn across the bottom. The line will provide a guide on which to write their text. After the text is written in, invite the children to illustrate their pages and sign their names.

- If the children choose to work on the alphabet books independently, encourage the children to keep track of all their ideas in a spiral notebook. Have the children share their thoughts with the class.

Rich has a rake.

Aardvarks are angry.
Bees like to buzz.
Carrots can't cough.
Daisies dance.

Challenge

Children who are writers (even in the early stages of writing) can develop full or partial lists of alphabetical words. Distribute pieces of paper with the letters of the alphabet printed vertically along the left edges of the paper. Ask the children to print a word for each letter. You may wish to give the children several days to complete their lists or a limited time period of 10 to 20 minutes. If the children are given a limited amount of time, let them know that they are only to complete as much of the list as they can in the time allotted. Incomplete lists are acceptable. The goal is to make children aware of alphabetical order.

At the end of the time period, call the group together to compare word lists. Words from the lists can be categorized into four basic groups—naming words (nouns), describing words (adjectives and adverbs), action words (verbs), and miscellaneous words. This activity in the lower levels will illustrate for younger children that there are different kinds of words that have different kinds of jobs. At the upper primary levels, the children will start to become aware of the different parts of speech and their uses.

Use these word lists to create sentences. Write one letter on the chart and have each child come up and write his or her word for the specified letter. Make sentences from the lists of words. If necessary, words can be added to the list through brainstorming (e.g., Fat funny foxes fish for French fries).

B
balls
barns
bounce
behind
Billy

Billy bounces balls behind barns.

Unit 3: Books Based on Reading Skills

About Books Based on Reading Skills

Writing classroom books provides an interesting option for teaching basic reading skills to primary-grade students. Reading skills books help children learn necessary skills without the constraints of a basal reader or a workbook. The children become active participants and are quickly immersed in brainstorming and researching words that are appropriate for the books under development. Without even being aware of it, children will learn a particular skill by using common sense and logic to determine which words will or will not be applicable. For example, if the children are brainstorming words for a book based on "long a" sounds, they will soon realize that not all words containing the letter "a" will be appropriate. If the words are further categorized into the different "long a" spellings, children will also learn the different vowel patterns for "long a" words, such as "ai" and "ay."

Books based on reading skills can be completed in a relatively short period of time. For younger children, the books can consist of examples of words that represent a certain reading skill, such as the "long e" sound or short vowels. Books based on reading skills can be composed of several short sentences that use a specific skill to describe or relate information about a topic or main character. The text does not necessarily have to develop a plot or resolve a conflict. The purpose of writing a reading skills book is to select text that uses and repeats concrete examples of the skill under development.

Getting Started

Books based on reading skills do not require a great deal of preparation. First help children choose a specific skill to work on.

Refer to the suggested topics on pages 30-32 for ideas. All skill books are created in a similar manner, however, the format may vary from book to book.

Present participle books are the easiest to write and require only one word of text per page. Have the children brainstorm action words (present participles) that describe a topic or main character. For example:

> Kites are…
> floating
> soaring
> flying
> diving

Digraph, blend, or opposites books will require brainstorming lists of words that relate to the skill that is the focus of the book. Samples for the *ch* digraph, for example, follow:

> *ch*air
> *ch*icks
> *ch*ew
> *ch*eese

Vowel books are easy to write and are an effective learning tool when pairs of rhyming words with the same vowel sound are used. The rhyming words can then be turned into nonsense sentences. For example:

> Long A
> Snakes have rakes.
> Trains have brains.
> Hay is made of clay.

Suggested Topics

The topics for reading skills books are vast—vowel sounds, digraphs, blends, opposites, contractions, and rhyming words, for example. Books based on reading skills may take a little more thought and creativity to integrate with some curriculum areas. Topics may be used individually or combined.

> Present Participle (*ing* words)—children choose words ending in *ing*. Each page of the book requires only one word.

Children are... laugh*ing*, sleep*ing*, sing*ing*, play*ing*.
Dogs are... bark*ing*, chas*ing*, scratch*ing*, runn*ing*.
Ships are... chugg*ing*, sail*ing*, glid*ing*, pull*ing*.

Digraphs (*ch, sh, th, wh*)—children choose words that begin with a specific digraph.

*Ch*icks on a *ch*air like to *ch*ew *ch*eese.
*Sh*arks at the *sh*ore like to *sh*ower on *sh*ips.
*Th*ree *th*rushes on a *th*rone like to *th*ink nice *th*oughts.
*Wh*ite *wh*ales *wh*o *wh*istle like to eat *wh*ite *wh*eat.

Blends—children choose words that begin with a specific blend or a combination of blends, such as *pl, sl, cl,* or *fl.*

*Pl*uto the *pl*atypus likes to *pl*ay with *pl*iers.
*Sl*y the *sl*ug likes to *sl*eep on a *sl*ide.
*Cl*ara the *cl*own likes to *cl*ose *cl*osets.
*Fl*ora the *fl*ower likes to *fl*y with *fl*amingoes.

Opposites—children write a story based on opposites.

Mr. Tall and Ms. Short
Mr. Tall likes daytime. Ms. Short likes nighttime.
Mr. Tall likes the upstairs. Ms. Short likes the downstairs.
Mr. Tall likes to stay inside. Ms. Short likes to go outside.

Chicks on a Chair By Room 1

Chicks on a Chair like to eat cherries with chocolate.

Vowels—children choose rhyming words based on specific vowel sounds. For example:

Long Vowels
A—Snakes have rakes.
E—Beagles look like eagles.
I—Mice eat ice.
O—Moles wear poles.
U—Suits are made of fruits.

Short Vowels
A—Cats wear hats.
E—Eggs grow legs.
I—Pigs wear wigs.
O—Frogs look like dogs.
U—Bugs have rugs.

Brainstorming/Prewriting Activities

The brainstorming/prewriting activities are probably the most critical component of the writing process. These activities help children prepare for the task of writing by providing the ideas and concepts required to actually write the classroom books. Charting children's ideas (on chart paper, butcher paper, or the bulletin board) provides the source from which the children choose ideas as they actually sit down and write their books or book pages. Use the following activities, as well as other activities that may appeal to you, to help children brainstorm and expand their ideas. Many options are provided here so that you may choose those that will be most appropriate for your class. Each activity can be used independently or combined with other activities to help children brainstorm text for their reading skills books.

Starting Point

Determine which skills you wish to focus on (see suggested topics on pages 30-32 for ideas). Help the children brainstorm as many words as they can think of during a 15-20 minute period. List all the brainstormed words on chart paper. Leave the list of words posted in a prominent location in the classroom for several days.

Use a variety of primary dictionaries from the school library or encourage the students to bring in their own dictionaries from home. Have the children work together in small groups to find words that may be added to the list. If the majority of children are non-readers, you may choose to read words from the dictionary and ask the children to help decide whether or not the words would be appropriate for their books.

Have the children look through the list for any words that could be used for the main character of the book. Circle words that are appropriate—for example, if writing a book on the *ch* digraph, children may choose the words *Charlie, chick, chimpanzee,* or *chipmunk.*

The children may have some initial difficulty in forming sentences. If this is the case, guided discussion will help to establish appropriate text.

> What would chicks chew?
> Could chicks play chess?
> Who could they play with?

Through trial and error, children's group efforts will eventually result in forming appropriate sentences. Children will also realize that while they may not be able to use every word on the list, some words can be used more than once. The charted list will later become the text for the children's book pages.

Skill Tree

Cut a large tree shape out of brown construction paper and attach it to a bulletin board. Cut green construction paper in the shape of leaves. Write one word on each leaf as an example of the skill being taught. The leaves for the tree might contain all contractions, long vowels, short vowels, pairs of opposites, and so on. The words can be changed each month to correspond with new skill lessons. Have the children help in cutting out the leaf shapes and selecting appropriate words. Invite children to use examples from the skill tree for the text of their reading skills book (see "Starting Point" on page 32). Examples for the "long e" sound might include (see illustration):

Mini-Books

Provide the children with four or five pieces of paper that have been folded in half and stapled into a book. Have the children think of words to include in their books, such as words with the "long e" sound. List the words the children suggest on a chart. Then have each child choose his or her favorite words from the chart and copy each word on a separate page of his or her mini-book. Invite the children to draw pictures of each word as well. For the "long e" sound, for example, the easiest words to illustrate might be:

> bee
> me
> tree
> he

Skill Butterflies

Skill butterflies are useful when teaching a skill that requires words to be paired together. For example:

> opposites—hot and cold
> contractions—don't and do not
> rhyming words—cake and rake

Give each child a butterfly outline on colored construction paper. Draw a line on each wing where the children can write their two skill words. Encourage the children to name all the words they can think of for a particular skill. Record the children's responses on chart paper. Have each child choose one example for his or her skill butterfly. Ask the children to write one word on the left wing and the corresponding word on the right wing. When completed, the butterflies may be placed on a skill tree bulletin board.

Poetry

Copy a new poem each week on large chart paper. The poem may be about the seasons, holidays, or an appropriate curriculum or content area. Give the children a few days to become familiar with the poem by reciting it together in class. Try using a pointer to assist the children in reading each word. Give the children the opportunity to take turns with the pointer and lead their classmates in reciting the poem as well.

When the children feel comfortable reading and reciting the poem, show the children any appropriate skill words. Use crayons or markers to circle the words that fall into specific skill categories. For example, all rhyming words might be circled in red, words beginning with blends circled in blue, and contractions circled in green. Concentrate on learning one skill at a time to avoid confusion. Help the children find the words that are pertinent to each skill they are studying. Use this method only if it is appropriate for the skill level of the children. Invite the children to use the skill words found in the poem for the text of their reading skills books (see "Starting Point" on page 32).

Have the children work with the poem for several days. Then provide them with a copy of the poem to take home and read to their parents or guardians. Encourage the children to illustrate the poem, too.

One balloon is red.
Another balloon is blue.
You are my friend.
I'll give one to you.

Sentence Strips

Divide the class into small groups. Give each group a strip of paper with a different skill word printed on the back. Ask each group to write a sentence using the assigned word skill. Tape the completed strips on the chalkboard. Have the other children find the skill words used by their classmates. This teaches the children to become their own editors and reinforces the skills that are being taught. For example:

Blends
I *pl*ayed in the yard.
That flower is *pl*astic.
*Pl*ease take out the garbage.

Adapt this activity for younger children by writing several simple skill words on the backs of large index cards. For rhyming words, for example, you might write *go, low,* and *toe.* As a class, read the words and encourage the children to dictate several sentences using the skill words in question. Write the sentences on the chalkboard. Invite the children to practice reading the sentences. For example:

Tim stepped on my *toe.*
To recess we will *go.*

Invite the children to use the sentence strips for the text of their reading skills books, if they wish.

Bringing It All Together

The following steps help children incorporate all of the preceding activities as they write and illustrate their book or books.

1. Help children make a title page for the book that includes the title of the book, class name, and date.

2. Give each child clean sheets of writing or drawing paper for his or her reading skills book pages.

3. Help each child copy his or her reading skills sentence from the brainstorming and charting sessions on the bottom of his or her page.

4. Have the children work individually or in small groups to illustrate the story pages (see pages 61-68 for illustrating ideas). Help children make the drawings as easy to identify as possible.

5. Make an author page and ask each child to sign his or her name. Include the author page at the beginning of the book.

6. Staple the pages of the book together with the title page on top. Or you may want to punch holes in the pages along the side or the top and tie the book together with string or yarn.

7. If you wish, help the children make a cover for the class book. You can use a variety of materials, such as cardboard, tagboard, fabric, and so on.

Expanding

- Children may have some initial difficulty in forming sentences. If this is the case, ask questions that are appropriate for the text. Encourage the children to use some of the words more than once, if necessary. The text for a book based on reading skills does not necessarily need a plot. The book is usually composed of several sentences about a main character or topic. The purpose is to try to integrate as many skill words as possible from the children's list. Skill books will vary in length. The books are complete when as many words as possible have been used.

- Encourage children at the upper primary levels to copy their entire lines of text independently. Give each child a sheet of paper with a line drawn across the bottom. The line will provide a guide on which to write the text. After the text is written, invite the children to illustrate their pages.

- If the children choose to work on the reading skills books independently, encourage the children to keep track of all their ideas in a spiral notebook. Have the children share their thoughts with the class.

Challenge

Children with stronger writing skills may want to copy the text into their own mini-books and then illustrate the pages themselves. Give each child several pieces of paper. Invite each child to choose one of the reading skills for his or her book. Or, you may want children to work in small groups. Encourage children to write the text they have come up with on the bottoms of their pages. Act as editor and advisor for the children. Then invite the children to illustrate each page as they wish. Staple each child's pages together to make a small book.

Unit 4: Fiction Books

About Fiction Books

Fiction books are an important addition to every classroom library. Unlike alphabet books or comparison books, writing a fiction book requires the use of more advanced thinking skills. Children quickly become aware of the need for continuity in story description and a logical progression for plot development. Children who have participated in brainstorming activities and written group fiction books before may be ready for independent fiction book writing.

Children love hearing and telling stories. Writing fiction books gives children the opportunity to use their imaginations freely to tell stories of their own. Children may want to illustrate their stories before, during, or after they write the story text. There is no set format. Writing fiction encourages individuality and creativity in the children.

Fiction books can be written both as a class or individually, whichever is appropriate for the children in your classroom.

Getting Started

Help children select a topic for the fiction book. Refer to the suggested topics on pages 40-42 for ideas. Particularly for younger children, it is important that the storyline be simple with only one or two characters that the children can easily relate to. The beginning, middle, and end of the story can all be formulated through group brainstorming sessions.

Upper primary children or those children who have had experience writing stories may wish to generate their own complete text from beginning to end. If necessary, suggest a topic and help the children think of characters, settings, and story problems.

Suggested Topics

Fiction books can be written about countless characters and subjects and easily integrated into most curriculum areas. The topics listed below are only a sampling of available themes.

Topics can be changed and personalized by the children as appropriate. Questions that help children focus on the beginning (B), middle (M), and end (E) for each topic are also provided as examples.

The Runaway Kite

    B— Someone is flying a kite when the wind blows it away.

    M— Where does the kite fly?

    E— What happens to the kite when it lands?

The Musical Bear

    B— A bear loves music and wants to be a violinist. All of the bear's friends laugh at him.

    M— Where does the bear go to practice? Who does he practice for?

    E— What happens to the bear after a year of practice? Does he give up? Does he achieve his dream?

The Train Trip

    B— A little boy is going to his grandparents for the summer. He doesn't want to leave his family and friends, but the train trip takes his mind off his problems.

    M— What does he see from the window of the train? What is going on inside the train?

    E— What happens when he arrives at the station? Does he run away? Does he get lost? Is he happy to see his grandparents?

Tommy Turtle

B— Tommy Turtle never listens to his parents
and is always getting into trouble.
One day he runs away.

M— Where does he go?
What other animals does he see?
What does he do to get into more trouble?

E— What happens to Tommy?
Does he learn a lesson?
Does he help someone?
How does he get back home?

The High-Flying Balloon

B— A clown is selling balloons at the circus.
She sneezes and lets go of the balloons
and they drift away.

M— Where do the balloons go?

E— What happens to the balloons?
Do they land?
Where do they land?
Do they get caught somewhere?
Does someone find the balloons?

Space Adventure
    B— Ms. Mackie's class takes a trip to Saturn.
    M— What do the children see on their trip?
    E— What happened to the class?
        Did they decide to stay on Saturn?
        What did they bring back from outerspace?

Monkey Fun
    B— The elephants in the jungle were very sad.
        Their best friends were the monkeys.
        The monkeys tried to cheer them up.
    M— What did the monkeys do to make the
        elephants laugh?
    E— Did the elephants finally laugh?
        What made them laugh?

The Late Robin
    B— All the robins left Florida after the winter,
        except for one robin. She finally decides
        to make the journey alone.
    M— What signs of spring did the robin see on her trip?
        What other sights did she see?
    E— What happened when the robin finally returned
        to her family?

Chicken Pox
    B— Patty has the chicken pox and can't play
        with any of her friends. She is very bored.
    M— What does Patty daydream about?
        Does she daydream about going somewhere?
        Does she daydream about being someone special?
    E— What happens to Patty when she feels better?

Brainstorming/Prewriting Activities

The brainstorming/prewriting activities are probably the most critical component of the writing process. These activities help children prepare for the task of writing by providing the ideas and concepts required to actually write the classroom books. Charting children's ideas (on chart paper, butcher paper, or the bulletin board) provides the source from which the children choose ideas as they actually sit down and write their books or book pages. Use the following activities, as well as other activities that may appeal to you, to help children brainstorm and expand their ideas.

● ● ● ● ● ● ● ● ● ● ● ● ● ● ●

Many options are provided here so that you may choose those that will be most appropriate for your class. Each activity can be used independently or combined with other activities to help children brainstorm text for their fiction books.

Starting Point

Most fiction books follow a simple three-part format—beginning, middle, and end. The beginning of a fiction book usually creates a setting and introduces a main character or characters. Brainstorm with the children possible settings and main characters for a story. Record the children's responses on chart paper. As a class, choose the main characters and where the story will take place.

You may want to help young children by writing a beginning for the class. Or, have the children think of their own ideas for a beginning during a group brainstorming session. For example, you might provide the following:

> One warm, windy day in March, I flew my kite from the top of the highest hill. It flew higher and higher until suddenly—the wind pulled the kite out of my hand. I watched my kite fly out of sight and wondered where it would go. It flew over...

Then help the children use their imaginations by asking them to close their eyes and visualize ideas for the middle of the story or stories. For example, using the beginning of the story about a kite, ask children to pretend they are watching the kite fly away. Then ask the children where they imagine the kite is flying. Ask each child for a response. Write the children's responses on chart paper. Help the children create complete sentences. This activity represents brainstorming the middle section of the story.

The end of a fiction book often provides a resolution to a conflict. Have the class work together to brainstorm an ending for the book. A combination of ideas can provide a good ending. Try to keep the ending simple. Here's an example of questions to ask to help brainstorm an ending to the kite story:

> The Runaway Kite
> Where would the kite land?
> Who would find the kite?
> What would the character or
> characters do with the kite once found?

List all of the children's suggestions for all three sections on chart paper. The charted list will later become the text for the children's book pages. Make sure the children's responses are in complete sentences. Have the children vote on their favorite sentences.

Reading Fiction Books

Storytime in the classroom can serve many purposes. Children listen for pleasure and at the same time can be taught important critical-thinking skills. Read *The Giving Tree* (see the bibliography on page 73) to the children. Discussions during and after the reading of a book will help children identify the three main components of most fiction stories—the beginning, the middle, and the end. Children may get ideas for their book pages from the selected books read in class. Chart the children's ideas.

Story Webbing and Mapping

After reading a book to the children, use the chalkboard or large chart paper to identify the characters, settings, and story events. Story mapping and webbing provides visual reinforcement of the three main components of most fiction books. Help the children chart their ideas as complete sentences. (See "Starting Point" on page 43.)

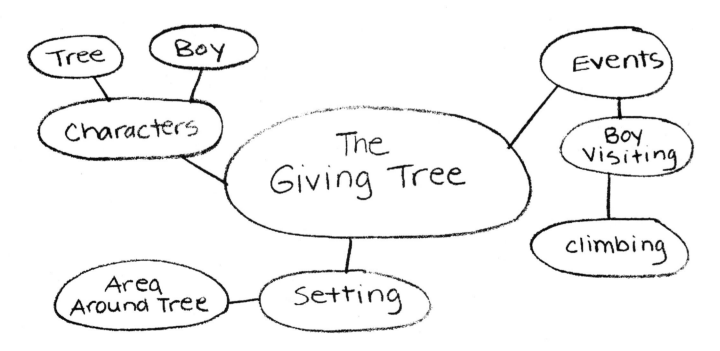

Brainstorm New Endings and Solutions

After reading a story, such as *Goldilocks and The Three Bears*, discuss the beginning, middle, and end of the story. Then have the children work together to brainstorm other possible solutions for the story ending. Several endings can be chosen and the story can be rewritten or retold by the group. For example:

> Goldilocks decides to stay with the three bears and teaches them how to make pepperoni pizza.

Goldilocks and The Three Bears

Create Story Murals

Cover a bulletin board with white paper. Have the children work together to illustrate their favorite class book. Each part of the book can be illustrated separately or the story can be illustrated in one continuous mural. (See "Starting Point" on page 43 for writing a beginning, middle, and end for the stories.)

Pictures to Brainstorm Original Fiction Stories

Invite children to cut pictures from magazines, old books, or calendars. Use the pictures as a catalyst for developing short fiction stories during brainstorming sessions. (See "Starting Point" on page 43.) For example, a picture of a cow in a meadow may generate the following discussion:

> Where is the setting (meadow)?
> Who is the main character (cow)?
> What can we name the cow (Sparky)?
> Describe the cow (brown and white spots, silky hide, long tail).

What problem might the cow have?
(She is all alone and can't find her friends.)
How can we solve the problem? (It is her
birthday and her friends are planning a
surprise party for her. When she goes back
to the barn, she'll find her friends and the party.)

Bringing It All Together

The following steps help children incorporate all of the preceding activities as they write and illustrate their fiction book or books.

1. If writing a book as a class, decide on a title. Help children make a title page for the book that includes the title of the book, class name, and date.

2. Give each child clean sheets of writing or drawing paper for his or her fiction book pages.

3. Help the children copy their sentences from the brainstorming and charting sessions on the bottom of their sheets of paper.

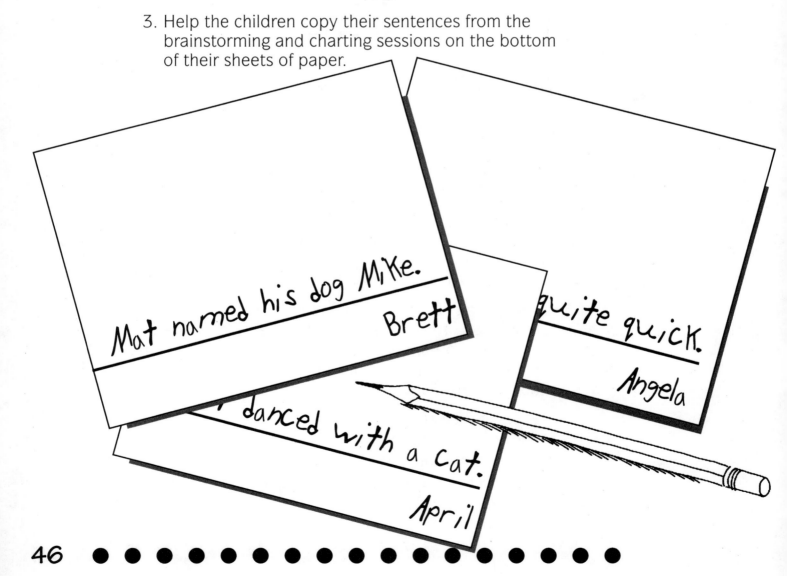

At the very earliest stage of writing, it may be necessary for you to print the text for the children. Ask each child to read his or her line of text with you as it is written on the page.

4. Encourage the children to illustrate their ideas (see pages 61-68 for illustrating ideas). Help children make the drawings as easy to identify as possible.

5. Have the children sign their names on their pages.

6. Staple the pages of the book together with the title page on top. Or you may want to punch holes in the pages along the side or the top and tie the book together using string or yarn.

7. If you wish, help the children make a cover for the class book. You can use a variety of materials, such as cardboard, tagboard, and so on.

Expanding

Encourage the use of colorful and descriptive language when writing. For example, a student may say "The kite is flying over some trees." Ask the child to describe the trees or name a specific type of tree. The expanded text may result in "The kite is flying over the beautiful pine trees."

Challenge

Help children write, illustrate, and "bind" their own stories. Follow the writing process in this chapter to help children come up with stories of their own. Act as advisor and editor for the children. When the children have completed their stories, help children "bind" their individual books.

Cut two pieces of tagboard the size of each child's pages of text. The books don't have to be in the traditional rectangular shape. Children may choose whatever shape they want that is workable. Glue fabric over the tagboard, making sure the fabric lies flat.

With markers, paints, or crayons, help the children write the titles of their stories on one of the pieces of covered tagboard. Help children write "By _____" on their books as well, inserting their names where appropriate. Children can also use other materials to decorate their book covers, such as fabric scraps, sequins, ribbon, and so on.

After the tagboard covers are dry, punch holes in the covers, as well as in each of the child's pages—either on the top, bottom, or one side. Make sure all the holes match each other on both the pages and each cover.

Place the text pages between the two covers and thread pieces of string, ribbon, yarn, or other tying material through the holes. Tie the strings together firmly. You may want to laminate the covers for durability.

Invite the children to take their books home to share with their families. Or, you may want to keep the books in the classroom library for the children to enjoy.

Unit 5: Nonfiction Books

About Nonfiction Books

Nonfiction books can be as simple or involved as is appropriate for the children in your classroom. Basic nonfiction books may be started at the early primary levels, while more in-depth books can be attempted when children have reached a more sophisticated level.

There are at least three types of nonfiction books that primary-grade children can create. The first involves children in the brainstorming and writing of books from their own experiences and prior knowledge. These books may be simple "All-About Books," such as books about the seasons, school, colors, or pets, or "How-To Books," such as how to plant seeds, set the table, blow up a balloon, ride a bike, or make a peanut butter and jelly sandwich. This type of book teaches children to write and correctly sequence facts. Also, these simple books help children differentiate between fact and fiction.

Another form of nonfiction writing combines children's prior knowledge and experience with the content and curriculum material they are studying in school. If children are studying insects, for instance, a good nonfiction book to write might be "All About Ants."

A third type of nonfiction book can be written from knowledge children gain from the curriculum and classroom instruction. The class may choose to write a biography about someone they have studied. For example, when studying about George Washington, children might wish to write a nonfiction book entitled "The Life of George Washington."

When nonfiction books are added to the classroom library, they provide the perfect introduction to a new curriculum unit. Child-created books are extremely effective learning tools because the vocabulary, sentence structure, content information, and illustrations are produced by the children.

Getting Started

Choose a topic for a class nonfiction book. Refer to the suggested topics on pages 51-52 for ideas. The information for a nonfiction book can be compiled using one of the following methods.

1. Use children's prior knowledge as material for simple nonfiction books.

   All About Our School
   All About Apples

2. Combine children's prior knowledge with information learned at school. For example, "All About Apples" might be written after a field trip to an apple orchard.

3. Or, children can write a class book about what they have learned during a unit of study, such as "All About Endangered Animals" or "How to Clean Up Our Community."

How to Clean Up
Our Community

1. Recycle

2. Pick up trash

3. Don't litter

4. Clean up
   after pets

Note: If a nonfiction book is being written at the beginning of the school year or with early primary children, writing should be simplified by choosing one of the first two methods. When children have some writing experience, you may want to use the third method and select a topic from a curriculum or content area. If this is the case, the book can be written as a culmination to the unit. This will ensure that children have maximum content knowledge before being asked to develop their text.

Suggested Topics

The list of topics for nonfiction books is endless, since nonfiction books can be integrated with any or all areas of the curriculum. The children working on these books benefit not only by improving their reading and writing skills, but also by learning content information from specific areas of the curriculum. The following are a few suggestions:

All About Our School
All About Colors
All About Our Community
All About Bike Safety
All About Playground Safety
All About Bus Safety
All About Class Rules
All About Manners
All About Community Helpers
All About Transportation
All About Families
All About Farms
All About Occupations
All About Apples
All About Fall
All About Fire Safety
All About Pumpkins
All About Thanksgiving
All About Indians
All About Winter
All About Hibernation
All About Winter Holidays
All About Snow

All About Winter Sports
All About Groundhogs
All About Our Presidents
All About Spring
All About Dinosaurs
All About Rain
All About Insects
All About Plants
All About Summer
All About the Zoo
How To Ride a Bike
How To Make a Sandwich
How To Take Care of Pets
How To Use the Library
How To Set the Table
How To Plant a Seed

Brainstorming/Prewriting Activities

The brainstorming/prewriting activities are probably the most critical component of the writing process. These activities help children prepare for the task of writing by providing the ideas and concepts required to actually write the classroom books. Charting children's ideas (on chart paper, butcher paper, or the bulletin board) provides the source from which the children choose ideas as they actually sit down and write their books or book pages. Use the following activities, as well as other activities that may appeal to you, to help children brainstorm and expand their ideas. Many options are provided here so that you may choose those that will be most appropriate for your class. Each activity can be used independently or combined with other activities to help children brainstorm text for their nonfiction books.

Starting Point

Write a title or topic at the top of a large sheet of chart paper. Let the children know that they are going to brainstorm the text for a nonfiction book based on their own experiences. The charted list will later become the text for the children's book pages. Begin brainstorming by asking the children to volunteer their thoughts about the topic listed. Accept all suggestions that make sense. Help children combine their thoughts and help one another develop interesting, complete sentences. For example, with a book entitled "All About Our School," the children might brainstorm the following text:

> We go to Parker Street School.
> Our school is very big.
> Ms. Johnson is our principal.

After the ideas have been charted, invite the class to brainstorm an appropriate ending. Even randomly sequenced text usually flows better if there is a sentence at the end that ties the text together. The class can choose their ending by reading and rereading their text and offering several possible conclusions. The children can vote for their favorite ending. For example, a culminating sentence for the book "All About School" could be:

> We have a great school!
> We love our school!

Create a Classroom Environment

Bring your curriculum to life by creating an interesting and stimulating classroom environment. Choose a topic for a class nonfiction book. Collect pictures, create bulletin boards, and encourage the children to bring nonfiction books, pictures, and artifacts from home that relate to the topic. The children can use the information collected to brainstorm text for their nonfiction books.

Field Trips

Field trips are an invaluable tool for collecting information for nonfiction books. Children are able to grasp concepts more readily when they are given the opportunity to learn through real-life experiences. It is difficult for a primary-grade child with limited knowledge to completely visualize an apple orchard or a farm from pictures in a book. However, when provided with the opportunity to visit one of these places, the experience becomes part of their foundation of knowledge.

Field trips do not have to be costly or time-consuming. A walk around the school building can provide a great deal of information for an "All About Our School" book. Depending upon the location of the school, a walking tour of the local neighborhood can provide ample material for a book about "Our Neighborhood." Short walks can also provide the subject matter for seasonal books, such as "All About Spring," "All About Summer," and so on. It doesn't matter where the location of the field trip takes you, the most important factor is the preparation for the trip. Let the children know where they are going and what they will be observing. When writing a book about the school, for example, the children can ask the following questions:

How many rooms are there in the school?
How many floors?
Where is the principal's office?
What does a principal do?

Ask the children to bring paper and pencils with them on the field trip and write or draw pictures of what they see. For nonwriters, bring a tape recorder on the field trip to record the children's responses. Let the children know that their observations and information will be used later to write a class book. After returning from the trip, meet with the group to discuss their observations. Record the children's thoughts and facts on a chart for the entire class to read.

Guest Speakers

Ask people from the community to be guest speakers in your classroom. The police department, fire department, post office, or local businesses, such as a bakery, grocery store, or bank, are often willing to send representatives to schools to speak with children about their jobs. Have the children prepare a list of questions they can ask the speakers before they arrive.

What do you do on your job?
What do you like best about your job?
What kind of training do you need to do your job?

Children can use the information they learn to brainstorm sentences for a nonfiction book about occupations or other appropriate topics.

Sequencing Activities

Nonfiction writing often requires events to be sequenced in a correct and logical order. Children can be taught sequencing using a variety of techniques.

- Provide the children with a variety of sizes of objects, such as cardboard boxes or balls. Encourage the group to arrange the items in order from smallest to largest.

- Write three simple sentences on strips of paper. Have the class arrange the strips in the correct sequential order. For example:

   The cat is hungry.
   Tom gets the cat food.
   The cat eats.

- Keep a magazine picture folder for use in the classroom. Find three pictures that illustrate an actual sequence of events, such as an egg, a baby chick, and an adult chicken. Point out the importance of events occurring in sequential order. Encourage the children to find other pictures to arrange in sequence as well. Discuss with the children why the sequence of events is important to a story. What happens if you read a picturebook or story backwards?

Invite children to brainstorm text for a nonfiction book using the sequencing techniques described here.

Nonfiction Reading

Ask the children to list nonfiction topics they are interested in, such as dinosaurs or space travel. Read several primary-level nonfiction books to the class (see the bibliography on pages 75-79). Discuss the differences between fiction and nonfiction. Children may get their ideas for their book pages from the selected books read in class. Chart the children's suggestions.

Bringing It All Together

The following steps help children incorporate all of the preceding activities as they write and illustrate their nonfiction book or books.

1. If writing a book as a class, decide on a title. Help children make a title page for the book that includes the title of the book, class name, and date.

2. Give each child clean sheets of writing or drawing paper for his or her non-fiction book pages.

3. Help the children copy their sentences from the brainstorming and charting sessions on the bottom of their sheets of paper. At the very earliest stage of writing, it may be necessary for you to print each line of text. Ask the children to read the text with you as it is written on the page.

4. Suggest a number of pages for the book. It is not necessary that each child have his or her own page to illustrate. Encourage small groups to work together to illustrate the pages (see pages 61-68 for illustrating ideas). The cover and title page can each be considered a page in the book as well.

5. Number each page of text in the lower right-hand corner.

6. Make an author page and ask each child to sign his or her name. Include the author page at the beginning of the story.

7. Staple the pages of the book together with the title page on top. Or you may want to punch holes in the pages along the side or the top and tie the book together using string or yarn.

8. If you wish, help the children make a cover for the class book. You can use a variety of materials, such as cardboard, tagboard, and so on.

Expanding

- You may want to divide several sentences of the nonfiction book into two or more segments for illustration. For example, the sentence "Apples can be red, green, or yellow" could be divided into four different pages.

- Children at the upper primary levels with more fully developed writing skills may enjoy working in groups to brainstorm and write individual chapters for a longer nonfiction book. For example, if the topic of a book is all about seasons, the class can be divided into four groups. Each group can write and illustrate a chapter about one of the four seasons.

Challenge

Many nonfiction books require a logical and specific sequence. For this reason, these books need to be approached somewhat differently. It would not make sense to write about picking apples and making applesauce before writing about planting the seeds, for example.

Use large chart paper to draw a simple web of the children's ideas on a specific topic. This is important, even if the children are nonreaders, because it helps them understand that many books cannot be written until the facts are sequenced in a logical order. A web for "All About Apples" might look like this:

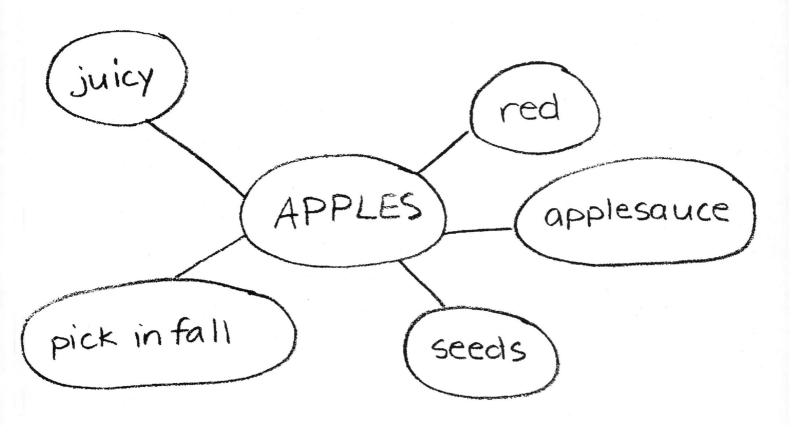

After the web has been completed, give the children time to become familiar with the information presented. When reviewing the web, the children will often point out that they have omitted certain facts that may need to be added. They may also find they have more information than they need and that some of the facts may not be of interest.

It may be necessary to direct the children's attention to the fact that they may need more information. The sample web on page 57 mentions the fall season, but does not include any information about the spring, summer, and winter seasons. Point out the omission and ask the class to add the appropriate information. A revised web might look like this:

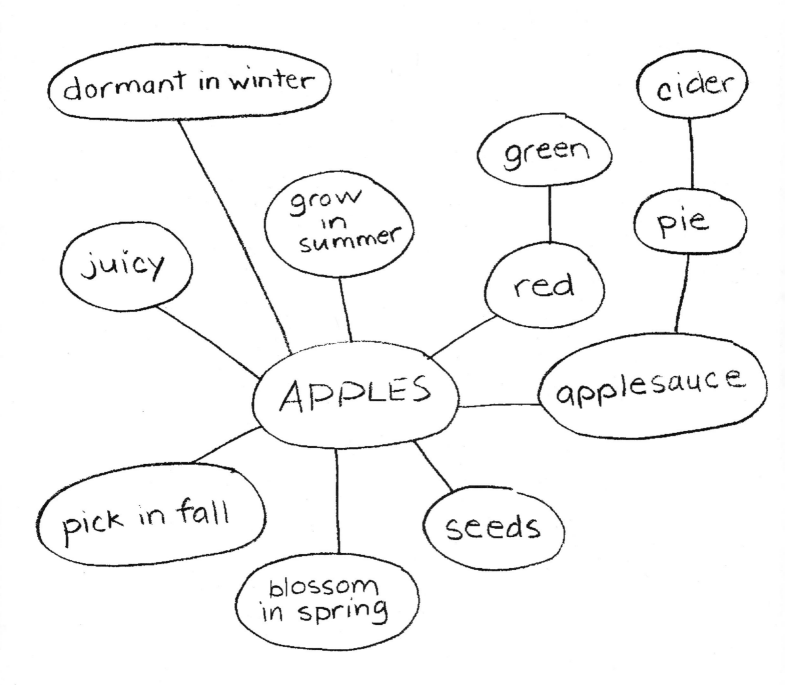

After editing the web, demonstrate to the class the importance of sequencing the text into a logical order. If the facts from the web were selected randomly, the book might read:

Applesauce, cider, and pies are made from apples.
We pick apples in the fall.
Apples are juicy.
Apples grow from seeds.
Blossoms grow in the spring.

Point out to the class that this text does not make sense because it is not in logical order.

Using a different-colored marker, ask the class to help number the facts on the web in a logical and consecutive order. Help the children write a beginning sentence from the web and then build the text in a logical progression.

4. Applesauce, cider, and pies are made from apples.

3. We pick apples in the fall.

5. Apples are juicy.

1. Apples grow from seeds.

2. Blossoms grow in the spring.

Use large chart paper on which to write the sentences that are developed from the web. Number the left-hand margin of the chart paper to correspond with the numbered items. Numbering the sentences will help the children remember to keep events in logical order.

Locate the number "1" on the web. Help the children read the word or phrase associated with this numeral. On the sample web about apples, for example, "seeds" may be labeled "number 1." Tell the children that "seeds" is not a sentence, but a topic. Ask a volunteer to create a sentence about seeds. Children will quickly learn the difference between phrases and complete sentences. This skill becomes an invaluable tool for later independent writing.

Ask the children to brainstorm as a group and help one another in developing interesting sentences about the topic. One child may offer "Apple seeds are tiny." Another may add "Apple trees grow from seeds." The children's sentences can be combined to read "Apple trees grow from tiny seeds."

Continue to chart each sentence in a similar manner until all phrases on the web have been charted into sentences.

When charting a nonfiction book from a web, the text does not have to be extensive. Nonfiction books do not necessarily require a sentence from every child in the class. Each sentence can later be divided into two or more components, giving each child a page to illustrate.

Read the completed chart with the class. Let the children help decide if additional sentences should be added. Encourage the children to agree on an ending for the book. Encourage the children to listen to everyone's suggestion and then vote on a favorite. The end of a book need not be complex. It can be as simple as "We love apples!"

We love apples!

Illustrating Ideas

About Illustrating Ideas

Illustrations are a vital component of books written by children. Early primary children are often not able to "read" their books, thus illustrations on each page are of even more importance. Illustrations help children associate written words with pictures and also teach children the importance of using picture clues to help them as they read.

Classroom books can be illustrated using crayons, pastels, cut paper, fingerpaints, watercolors, magazine pictures, stencils, and so on. Encourage children to choose one method or a combination of materials and methods to illustrate their class books. However, it is generally a good idea to keep first attempts at illustrating relatively simple. Children are often anxious to see their finished products. Some of the more involved techniques prolong bookmaking and may not be appropriate for young children. Crayon illustrations are a good way to begin the illustrating process.

It is important for each child to write his or her name on his or her illustrated pages. Signing the page not only gives the children ownership, but more importantly, a great sense of accomplishment.

Pre-Illustrating Activities

- Collect pictures of animals, people, and scenes. Discuss the pictures with the children and have them look at the pictures in detail in group discussions. For example, show the class a picture of a cat. Then ask the following questions:

   What color is the cat's fur?
   How many legs does the cat have?
   What color is the cat's eyes?

Although the questions are obvious and the children will be able to answer them immediately, this activity helps them recognize the importance of adding detail to a drawing.

- Provide models of objects for the children to draw. Pictures can be found in primary dictionaries, encyclopedias, and magazines.

- Help children determine shapes they should use to create interesting illustrations. Refer to the sample illustrations on pages 63-64. When showing children how to draw figures, use a piece of scratch paper or the chalkboard. Separate the figure into several simple shapes. For example, a cat can be drawn from one circle, one oval, and two triangles.

- Encourage the children to practice drawing several pictures. Provide each child with a large piece of drawing paper. Give each child time to use simple shapes to create illustrations.

Preparing a Book for Illustration

Books can be made easily in the classroom. Rectangular-shaped books are the simplest to prepare and assemble. However, books can also be cut into a shape that is consistent with the topic of a book. For example, "An Apple Is As Red As..." could be cut in the shape of an apple.

If books are cut in a shape other than a rectangle or square, be sure to leave one side of the book with a straight edge to allow for binding. The straight edge can be left along the traditional left-hand side of the book, the top, or the bottom.

If a book includes cut-paper illustrations, it is a good idea to have the pages laminated. The lamination prevents damage to the illustrations and creates a very durable book.

Sample Illustrations

Cat

1 circle
1 oval
2 triangles

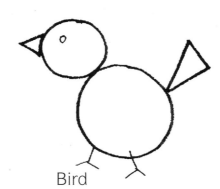

Bird

2 circles
2 triangles

Girl

1 circle
1 letter A

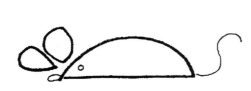

Mouse

1/2 oval
2 teardrops

Butterfly

1 circle
1 oval
2 letter B's

Boy

1 circle
1 letter X

Rabbit

2 circles
3 ovals
2 teardrops

Turtle

1 circle
1 letter D
4 letters U's

Kangaroo

1 number 5

Duck

1 letter G

Bear

4 circles
1 oval
4 letter U's

Hippo

1 peanut shape
1 oval
4 letter U's

Penguin

1 number 8
1 oval

Caterpillar

6 circles

Fish

1 eye shape
1 moon shape

Snake

1 number 6

Elephant

1 number 90
1 oval
4 letter U's

Parrot

1 number 3
1 circle
3 heart shapes

Stencil Art

Stencil art is an interesting technique for illustrating books with children. Since it is very difficult for young children to duplicate a picture when drawing or cutting freehand, the use of stencils simplifies the illustrating process.

Stencils can be purchased commercially or made by the children themselves. Provide children with cardboard or oaktag when making their own stencils. Children can practice drawing the characters or figures, transfer the drawings to oaktag, and then cut the stencils out. In classrooms of younger children, you or an adult helper can help prepare stencils for the students. Stencils should be stored in an envelope or safe place until they are needed.

Stencils can be made for any object or figure that appears on more than one page of a book. Settings often remain unchanged throughout a book. Therefore, it would be helpful to create stencils for some of the basic "scenery." An outdoor setting may require stencils for clouds, trees, the sun, and flowers, for example. An indoor setting may require stencils for beds, chairs, tables, and windows. Stencil illustrations can be created with crayon, cut paper, or a combination of both.

Crayon Stencils

Have the children trace their stencil shapes with a pencil, crayon, or marker directly onto the page of the book they are illustrating. To add interest to the illustration, have the children draw outlines of pictures, such as flowers, birds, or butterflies, using pencils, crayons, or markers.

Ask the children to complete the illustrations by coloring the outlined figures with crayon.

Cut-Paper Stencils

Work with a small group of children at an illustrating table. Ask each child to cut out a character or object using the prepared stencils and colored construction paper.

Arrange the stenciled figures on a page of the book. Have the children draw and cut out any additional figures that may be needed to complete the picture, such as grass, water, a bird, a butterfly, or the sun. Then have the children arrange the figures on the page and glue them in place. A glue stick works well and helps prevent getting too much glue on the cutouts.

Cut-Paper Illustrations

Cut-paper illustrations are an alternative method of illustrating books. Pictures made from colored construction paper are vibrant and elegantly simple. They use the same basic shapes as crayon illustrations, but give the children the opportunity to work with a different medium.

Children will have greater success with this technique if they have already illustrated books using crayons. The experience with using crayons will not only help refine their fine-motor skills, but at the same time, give the children practice drawing the figures they will eventually be cutting out.

Prepare a table in the room for illustrating. Equip the table with a large box of colored construction paper, wallpaper, tissue paper, aluminum foil, scissors, pencils, and glue or paste. Glue sticks are convenient for this type of project.

Work with small groups of children at the table. A group should consist of about four or five illustrators.

Keep cut-paper illustrations simple. Too much detail is difficult to complete and may frustrate some children. Give each child a page of text to illustrate. Help the children draw their figures with pencil on the back of the construction paper, cut out the figures, and then turn the papers over so the pencil marks will not show. Start with the background. Cut strips of paper for water, grass, dirt, or roads, for example.

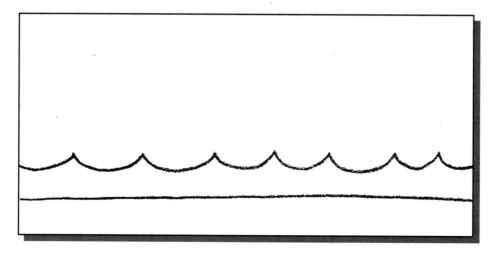

Fold a piece of construction paper in half and cut out two clouds. Then draw a sun or moon and cut this object out of construction paper as well.

Help children draw the main figure or figures for the illustration. After cutting out the characters, the details, such as the eyes and the nose, can also be cut out of colored construction paper. If a detail is too small to cut out, help children draw directly on the page with a fine-point marker. Each child should sign his or her page of work as well.

Whenever possible, cut-paper illustrations should be laminated upon completion. Lamination helps preserve the pictures and allows the children to read the books without pieces of the illustrations falling off.

A Final Word

Keep the completed books in a classroom library. Encourage the children in your classroom to read the books as often as they like. Not only will children learn new skills from their books, but they will also enjoy reading and re-reading their own creations!

Bibliography

Comparison Books

As: A Surfeit of Similes by Norton Juster. New York, NY: William Morrow, 1989.

Chickens Aren't the Only Ones by Ruth Heller. New York, NY: Grosset & Dunlap, 1981.

Red by Gabrielle Woolfitt. Minneapolis, MN: Carolrhoda Books, 1992.

Red Is Best by Kathy Stinson. Toronto, Canada: Annick Press, 1982.

More Similies by Joan Hanson. Minneapolis, MN: Lerner Publications, 1979.

Similes by Joan Hanson. Minneapolis, MN: Lerner Publications, 1976.

Alphabet Books

Alaska ABC Book by Charlene Kreeger and Shannon Cartwright. Wasilla, AK: Lone Raven Publishing, 1978.

All in the Woodland Early: An ABC Book by Jane Yolen. New York, NY: Putnam, 1979.

Alphabatics by Suse Macdonald. New York, NY: Bradbury, 1986.

The Alphabeast Book by Dick King-Smith. New York, NY: Macmillan, 1992.

Animalia by Graeme Base. New York, NY: Abrams, 1987.

Anno's Alphabet: An Adventure in Imagination by Mitsumasa Anno.

New York, NY: Harper & Row, 1975.

Antics! An Alphabetical Anthology by Cathi Hepworth. New York, NY: Putnam, 1992.

Ashanti to Zulu: African Traditions by Margaret Musgrove. New York, NY: Dial Books, 1976.

The Bird Alphabet Book by Jerry Pallotta. Watertown, MA: Charlesbridge, 1989.

Chicka Chicka Boom Boom by Bill Martin, Jr. New York, NY: Simon & Schuster, 1989.

An Edward Lear Alphabet by Edward Lear. New York, NY: Lothrop, Lee & Shepard, 1983.

The Flower Alphabet Book by Jerry Pallotta. Watertown, MA: Charlesbridge, 1989.

The Folks in the Valley: A Pennsylvania Dutch ABC by Jim Aylesworth. Scranton, PA: HarperCollins, 1992.

Fun from A to Z by J.T. Winik. Milwaukee, WI: Penworthy, 1985.

Geography from A to Z: A Picture Glossary by Jack Knowlton. New York, NY: Thomas Y. Crowell, 1988.

The Icky Bug Alphabet Book by Jerry Pallotta. Watertown, MA: Charlesbridge, 1989.

The Ocean Alphabet Book by Jerry Pallotta. Watertown, MA: Charlesbridge, 1989.

On Market Street by Arnold Lobel. New York, NY: Greenwillow Books, 1981.

Pigs from A to Z by Arthur Geisert. Boston, MA: Houghton Mifflin, 1986.

The Yucky Reptile Alphabet Book by Jerry Pallotta. Watertown, MA: Charlesbridge, 1990.

The Z Was Zapped: A Play in Twenty-Six Acts by Chris Van Allsburg. Boston, MA: Houghton Mifflin, 1987.

Books Based on Reading Skills

Antonyms by Joan Hanson. Minneapolis, MN: Lerner Publications, 1972.

Breakfast in the Afternoon by Cynthia Basil. New York, NY: William Morrow, 1979.

A Cache of Jewels and Other Collective Nouns by Ruth Heller. New York, NY: Grosset & Dunlap, 1987.

Dragon Kites and Dragonflies: A Collection of Chinese Nursery Rhymes by Demi. San Diego, CA: Harcourt Brace Jovanovich, 1986.

Horton Hears a Who! by Dr. Seuss. New York, NY: Random House, 1954.

Kites Sail High: A Book About Verbs by Ruth Heller. New York, NY: Grosset & Dunlap, 1988.

Many Luscious Lollipops: A Book About Adjectives by Ruth Heller. New York, NY: Grosset & Dunlap, 1989.

Merry-Go-Round: A Book About Nouns by Ruth Heller. New York, NY: Grosset & Dunlap, 1990.

Plurals by Joan Hanson. Minneapolis, MN: Lerner Publications, 1979.

Three Jovial Huntsmen by Susan Jeffers. New York, NY: Bradbury, 1973.

Tomie de Paola's Mother Goose by Tomie de Paola. New York, NY: Putnam, 1985.

Yertle the Turtle and Other Stories by Dr. Seuss. New York, NY: Random House, 1958.

Yes and No: A Book of Opposites by Richard Hefter. New York, NY: McGraw-Hill, 1975.

Fiction Books

Anna's Garden Songs by Mary Q. Steele. New York, NY: Greenwillow Books, 1989.

The Apple Bird by Brian Wildsmith. New York, NY: Oxford, 1987.

Apple Pigs by Ruth Orbach. New York, NY: Putnam, 1981.

Apple Tree Christmas by Trinka H. Noble. New York, NY: Dial Books, 1984.

Arthur's Christmas by Marc Brown. Boston, MA: Little, Brown, 1984.

Arthur's Halloween Costume by Lillian Hoban. New York, NY: Harper & Row, 1984.

Autumn Harvest by Alvin Tresselt. New York, NY: Lothrop, Lee & Shepard, 1951.

Bee My Valentine by Miriam Cohen. New York, NY: Greenwillow Books, 1978.

Big Kite Contest by Dorotha Ruthstrom. New York, NY: Pantheon, 1980.

The Boy Who Didn't Believe in Spring by Lucille Clifton. New York, NY: E. P. Dutton, 1973.

Brown Bear, Brown Bear What Do You See? by Bill Martin, Jr. New York, NY: Henry Holt and Co., 1983

Candy Witch by Steven Kroll. New York, NY: Holiday House, 1979.

A Christmas Feast: Poems, Sayings, Greetings, and Wishes by Edna Barth. Merlin, OR: Clarion, 1979.

Christmas Moon by Denys Cazet. New York, NY: Macmillan, 1988.

Christmas Tree Memories by Aliki. Scranton, PA: HarperCollins, 1991.

Cobweb Christmas by Shirley Climo. New York, NY: Harper & Row, 1982.

Cranberry Thanksgiving by Wende and Harry Devlin. New York, NY: Macmillan, 1990.

An Early American Christmas by Tomie de Paola. New York, NY: Holiday House, 1987.

Farmer Goff and His Turkey, Sam by Brian Schatell. New York, NY: Harper & Row, 1982.

Fire Cat by Esther Averill. New York, NY: Harper & Row, 1983.

Four Stories for Four Seasons by Tomie de Paola. Englewood Cliffs, NJ: Prentice Hall, 1977.

Freight Train by Donald Crews. New York, NY: Greenwillow Books, 1978.

The Giving Tree by Shel Silverstein. New York, NY: Harper & Row, 1964.

Great Valentine's Day Balloon Race by Adrienne Adams. New York, NY: Macmillan, 1980.

Green Eggs and Ham by Dr. Seuss. New York, NY: Random House Books for Young Children, 1960.

Here Comes the Strikeout by Leonard Kessler. New York, NY: Harper & Row, 1965.

Is It Red? Is It Yellow? Is It Blue? by Tana Hoban. New York, NY: Greenwillow Books, 1978.

It's Halloween by Jack Prelutsky. New York, NY: Greenwillow Books, 1977.

It's Really Christmas by Lillian Hoban. New York, NY: Greenwillow Books, 1982.

Johnny Appleseed: A Tall Tale by Steven Kellogg. New York, NY: William Morrow, 1988.

Johnny No Hit by Matt Christopher. Boston, MA: Little, Brown, 1977.

Leprechauns Never Lie by Lorna Balian. Nashville, TN: Abingdon, 1980.

Mary Wore Her Red Dress and Henry Wore His Green Sneakers by Merle Peek. Merlin, OR: Clarion, 1985.

Merrily Comes Our Harvest In: Poems for Thanksgiving edited by Lee Bennett Hopkins. San Diego, CA: Harcourt Brace Jovanovich, 1978.

The Mixed-Up Chameleon by Eric Carle. New York, NY: Harper & Row, 1984.

Mr. Rabbit and the Lovely Present by Charlotte Zolotow. New York, NY: Harper & Row, 1962.

The Mystery of the Flying Orange Pumpkin by Steven Kellogg. New York, NY: Dial Books, 1980.

The New House by Lorinda B. Cauley. San Diego, CA: Harcourt Brace Jovanovich, 1981.

One Tough Turkey by Steven Kroll. New York, NY: Holiday House, 1982.

The Polar Express by Chris Van Allsburg. Boston, MA: Houghton Mifflin, 1985.

Potato Pancakes All Around: A Hanukkah Tale by Marilyn Hirsh. New York, NY: Bonim Books, 1978.

Rain Makes Applesauce by Julian Scheer. New York, NY: Holiday House, 1964.

A Rainbow of My Own by Don Freeman. New York, NY: Penguin, 1978.

Shadow by Blaise Cendrars. New York, NY: Scribners, 1982.

Sleepy Bear by Lydia Dabcovich. New York, NY: E. P. Dutton, 1982.

Snow Parade by Barbara Brenner. Southbridge, MA: Crown, 1984.

The Snowman by Raymond Briggs. New York, NY: Random House, 1988.

Something Queer on Vacation by Elizabeth Levy. New York, NY: Dellacorte, 1980.

Thanksgiving Day by Gail Gibbons. New York, NY: Holiday House, 1983.

That Terrible Halloween Night by James Stevenson. New York, NY: Greenwillow Books, 1980.

Valentine Fantasy by Carolyn Haywood. New York, NY: William Morrow, 1976.

Vanishing Pumpkin by Tony Johnson. New York, NY: Putnam, 1984.

Wake Up Bear, It's Christmas by Steven Gammell. New York, NY: Lothrop, Lee & Shepard, 1981.

Who Stole the Apples? by Sigrid Heuck. New York, NY: Knopf, 1986.

Winter Barn by Peter Parnall. New York, NY: Macmillan, 1986.

Winter Place by Ruth Y. Radin. Boston, MA: Little, Brown, 1982.

A Woggle of Witches by Adrienne Adams. New York, NY: Macmillan, 1971.

Nonfiction Books

Ants Are Fun by Mildred Myrick. New York, NY: Harper & Row, 1968.

Ant Cities by Arthur Dorros. New York, NY: Harper & Row, 1987.

Apple Tree by Barrie Watts. Englewood Cliffs, NJ: Silver Burdett, 1987.

Apples: A Bushel of Fun & Facts by Bernice Kohn. New York, NY: Parents' Magazine Press, 1976.

Backyard Insects by Millicent Selsam and Ronald Goor. New York, NY: Four Winds Press, 1981.

Bean and Plant by Christine Back. Englewood Cliffs, NJ: Silver Burdett, 1986.

The Bee by Iliane Roels. New York, NY: Grosset & Dunlap, 1969.

Bread by Dorothy Turner. Minneapolis, MN: Carolrhoda Books, 1989.

Breathing by John Gaskin. New York, NY: Franklin Watts, 1984.

Bugs by George McGavin. New York, NY: Bookwright Press, 1989.

Bugs by Nancy Winslow Parker and Joan Richards Wright. New York, NY: Greenwillow Books, 1987.

Bugs, Bugs, Bugs by Sandra Granseth and Diana McMillen. Des Moines, IA: Meredith Corporation, 1989.

Butterflies and Moths by Keith Porter. New York, NY: Bookwright Press, 1986.

Catch a Cricket by Carla Stevens. Reading, MA: Addison-Wesley, 1961.

The Cloud Book by Tomie de Paola. New York, NY: Holiday House, 1975.

Disaster! Blizzards and Winter Weather by Dennis B. Fradin. Chicago, IL: Childrens Press, 1983.

Discovering Bugs by George McGavin. New York, NY: Bookwright Press, 1989.

Ears Are for Hearing by Paul Showers. New York, NY: Thomas Y. Crowell, 1990.

Eating by John Gaskin. New York, NY: Franklin Watts, 1984.

Every Kid's Guide to Nutrition and Health Care by Joy Berry. Chicago, IL: Childrens Press, 1987.

The Eye and Seeing by Steve Parker. New York, NY: Franklin Watts, 1989.

● ● ● ● ● ● ● ● ● ● ● ● ● ● ● ●

Flash, Crash, Rumble, and Roll by Franklyn M. Branley. New York, NY: Thomas Y. Crowell, 1985.

From Egg to Butterfly by Marlene Reidel. Minneapolis, MN: Carolrhoda Books, 1981.

Germs Make Me Sick! by Melvin Berger. New York, NY: Thomas Y. Crowell, 1985.

Good Plants Are Hard to Find by Roma Dehr and Ronald M. Bazar. Vancouver, B.C.: Earth Beat Press, 1989.

Health and Hygiene by Brian R. Ward. New York, NY: Franklin Watts, 1988.

The Healthy Habits Handbook by Slim Goodbody. New York, NY: Coward-McCann, 1983.

How the Forest Grew by William Jaspersohn. New York, NY: Greenwillow Books, 1980.

How to Grow a Jelly Glass Farm by Kathy Mandry. New York, NY: Pantheon Books, 1974.

The Human Body: The Heart by Kathleen Elgin. New York, NY: Franklin Watts, 1968.

Hurricane Watch by Franklyn M. Branley. New York, NY: Thomas Y. Crowell, 1985.

I Can Be a Weather Forecaster by Claire Martin. Chicago, IL: Childrens Press, 1987.

Insect Pets: Catching and Caring for Them by Carla Stevens. New York, NY: Greenwillow Books, 1978.

Insects by Jeanne Brouillette. Chicago, IL: Follett Publishing, 1963.

It's Easy to Have a Caterpillar Visit You by Caroline O'Hagan. New York, NY: Lothrop, Lee & Shepard, 1980.

Junk Food: What It Is, What It Does by Judith S. Seixas. New York, NY: Greenwillow Books, 1984.

A Kid's First Book of Gardening by Derek Fell. Philadelphia, PA: Running Press, 1990.

Let's Be Nature's Friends by Jack Stokes. New York, NY: Henry Z. Walck, Inc., 1977.

Lucky Ladybugs by Gladys Conklin. New York, NY: Holiday House, 1968.

Let's Find Out About Insects by David C. Knight. New York, NY: Franklin Watts, 1967.

Life of the Butterfly by Heiderose and Andreas Fischer-Nagel. Minneapolis, MN: Carolrhoda Books, 1987.

Meat by Elizabeth Clark. Minneapolis, MN: Carolrhoda Books, 1990.

Milk by Dorothy Turner. Minneapolis, MN: Carolrhoda Books, 1989.

Monarch Butterflies by Emilie Lepthien. Chicago, IL: Childrens Press, 1989.

The Mystery of Sleep by Alvin and Virginia Silverstein. Boston, MA: Little, Brown, 1987.

Nutrition by Leslie Jean LeMaster. Chicago, IL: Childrens Press, 1985.

Our Changing World: The Forest by David Bellamy. New York, NY: C. N. Potter, 1988.

Our Changing World: The River by David Bellamy. New York, NY: Crown, 1988.

Plant Experiments by Vera Webster. Chicago, IL: Childrens Press, 1982.

Potato by Barrie Watts. Englewood Cliffs, NJ: Silver Burdett, 1987.

Potatoes by Dorothy Turner. Minneapolis, MN: Carolrhoda Books, 1989.

Raindrops and Rainbows by Rose Wyler. Englewood Cliffs, NJ: Julian Messner, 1989.

Roots Are Food Finders by Franklyn M. Branley. New York, NY: Thomas Y. Crowell, 1975.

Science Fun with Peanuts and Popcorn by Rose Wyler. Englewood Cliffs, NJ: Julian Messner, 1986.

Seeds by Terry Jennings. New York, NY: Gloucester Press, 1988.

Seeds: Pop Stick Glide by Patricia Lauber. Southbridge, MA: Crown, 1981.

The Story of Your Ear by Alving and Virginia Silverstein. New York, NY: Coward-McCann, 1981.

Talkabout Growing by Henry Pluckrose. New York, NY: Franklin Watts, 1988.

Thinkabout Hearing by Henry Pluckrose. New York, NY: Franklin Watts, 1986.

Tornado Alert by Franklyn M. Branley. New York, NY: Thomas Y. Crowell, 1988.

Trash by Charlotte Wilcox. Minneapolis, MN: Carolrhoda Books, 1988.

Vegetables by Susan Wake. Minneapolis, MN: Carolrhoda Books, 1990.

Weather by Terry Jennings. New York, NY: Gloucester Press, 1988.

Weather Experiments by Vera R. Webster. Chicago, IL: Childrens Press, 1984.

Weather Forecasting by Gail Gibbons. New York, NY: Four Winds Press, 1987.

Weather Words and What They Mean by Gail Gibbons. New York, NY: Holiday House, 1990.

What Happens to a Hamburger? by Paul Showers. New York, NY: Thomas Y. Crowell, 1985.

What Will the Weather Be? by Linda DeWitt. New York, NY: HarperCollins, 1991.

What Will the Weather Be Like Today? by Paul Rogers. New York, NY: Greenwillow Books, 1990.

Wind and Weather by Judith Vigna. Niles, IL: Albert Whitman & Co., 1989.

Your First Garden Book by Marc Brown. Boston, MA: Little, Brown, 1981.

Your Heart and Blood by Leslie Jean LeMaster. Chicago, IL: Childrens Press, 1984.

Your Heart and Lungs by Dorothy Baldwin and Claire Lister. New York, NY: Bookwright Press, 1984.